What is phonics?

Phonics helps children learn to read and write by teaching them the letter sounds (known as phonemes), rather than the letter names, e.g. the sound that 'c' makes rather than its alphabetic name. They then learn how to blend the sounds: the process of saying the sounds in a word or 'sounding out' and then blending them together to make the word, for example c – a – t = cat. Once the phonemes and the skill of blending are learnt, children can tackle reading any phonetically decodable word they come across, even ones they don't know, with confidence and success.

However, there are of course many words in the English language that aren't phonetically decodable, e.g. if a child gets stuck on 'the' it doesn't help if they sound it out and blend it. We call these 'tricky words' and they are just taught as words that are so 'tricky' that children have to learn to recognise them by sight.

How do phonic readers work?

Phonic reading books are written especially for children who are beginning to learn phonics at nursery or school, and support any programme being used by providing plenty of practice as children develop the skills of decoding and blending. By targeting specific phonemes and tricky words, increasing in difficulty, they ensure systematic progression with reading.

Because phonic readers are primarily decodable – aside from the target tricky words which need to be learnt, children should be able to read the books with real assurance and accomplishment.

Big Cat phonic readers:
The Rainforest at Night

In Big Cat phonic readers the specific phonemes and tricky words being focussed on are highlighted here in these notes, so that you can be clear about what your child's learning and what they need to practise.

While reading at home together, there are all sorts of fun additional games you can play to help your child practise those phonemes and tricky words, which can be a nice way to familiarise yourselves with them before reading, or remind you of them after you've finished. In *The Rainforest at Night*, for example:

- the focus phonemes are aw (crawl), al (talk), are (care). Why not write them down and encourage your child to practise saying the sounds as you point to them in a random order. This is called 'Speed Sounds' and as you get faster and faster with your pointing, it encourages your child to say them as quickly as possible. You can try reversing the roles, so that you have a practice too!

- the tricky words are 'the', 'when', 'to', 'a', 'they', 'little', 'their', 'come', 'some', 'away', 'have' and 'so'. You can play 'Hide and Seek' by asking your child to close their eyes and count to 10, while you write each word on a piece of paper, hiding them somewhere in the room you're in or the garden for your child to find. As they find each one, they should try reading and spelling the word out.

Reading together

- Look at the front cover of The *Rainforest at Night* and talk about what you can see.

By looking at the picture, what do you think this book might be about?

Try sounding out the title. Can you read it?

What do you know about the rainforest? How might it be different at night?

- Enjoy reading *The Rainforest at Night* together, noticing the focus phonemes (aw, al, are) and tricky words (the, when, to, a, they, little, their, come, some, away, have, so). It's useful to point to each word as your child reads, and encouraging to give them lots of praise as they go.

- If your child gets stuck on a word, and it's phonetically decodable, encourage them to sound it out. You can practise blending by saying the sounds aloud a few times, getting quicker and quicker. If they still can't read it, tell them the word and move on.

Talking about the book

- Look at the pictures on pp18–19 and talk about the different creatures, which your favourite is and which you like the least.

- Practise the focus phonemes from *The Rainforest at Night* by asking your child to tell you which sound, for example, the word 'care' ends with, or to sound out some of the key words, for example, 'crawl'.

The Rainforest at Night

Written and photographed by Nic Bishop

Collins

When it gets dark in
the rainforest,
things start to happen.

Bats wake up and fly in the night. The bats sleep in the day under a leaf.

At night they zip and zoom in the sky to chase moths and insects. A bat can flip a moth into its mouth with its wings.

A hungry bat will eat a hundred insects in a night.

Lightning bugs wink and shine little lights. A lightning bug will flash its light to talk to other lightning bugs. It winks it on and off to say it is looking for a mate.

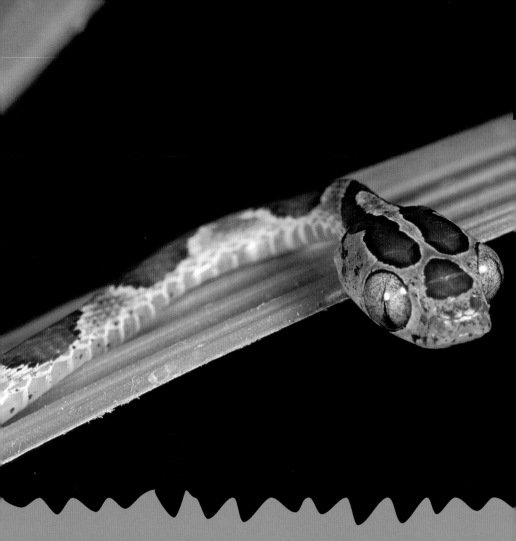

Snakes slide and sneak up on their food. Lots of snakes come out at night. Some hunt on the ground. Some slither up trees.

This snake eats tree frogs. It can see in the dark. If it sees a frog it sneaks up and grabs it in its mouth.

Frogs creep and crawl in the trees. This is a tree frog. It has sticky fingers to help it go up trees and it can see in the dark too.

It looks for moths, grasshoppers
and small insects to eat.
If a snake sneaks up on it, its
long legs help it leap away.

Grasshoppers come out to munch a leaf. Grasshoppers clamber in the trees at night. They feed on plants. They have long feelers, to help feel the way in the dark.

Frogs, bats and tarantulas eat grasshoppers, so they have to take care.

Tarantulas creep and peek out of their dens.

A tarantula sleeps in its den in the day. It crawls out at night. It stays still till something comes close. Then the tarantula grabs it and bites it with its fangs.

bats

bugs

frog

grasshopper

snake

tarantula

Getting creative

- Have some fun with your child by playing the game, 'Hot or Cold', where you write the focus phonemes on pieces of paper and hide them around the room for your child to find, giving 'hot' and 'cold' clues as they look. When your child finds them, encourage them to say the sound.

- To practise the tricky words, why not create some tricky-word anagrams for your child to unscramble, for example 'etyh' for 'they'.

- If your child's enjoyed *The Rainforest at Night* they might like to find out about other creatures who are active at night. They could do some research at the local library or using the internet and draw up an information sheet with pictures and key words.

- They could then compare creatures in the rainforest to creatures that they might see in their own local area, for example foxes, badgers, cats.

Other books at Level 2:

Fiction	Non-fiction
Zog and Zebra — Mal Peet and Elspeth Graham, Sarah Horne	**The Sun and the Moon** — Paul Shipton
A Day Out — Petr Horáček	**Gorillas** — Teresa Heapy
The Singing Beetle — Linda Strachan, Oliver Hurst	**The Rainforest at Night** — Nic Bishop

Collins Big Cat
Reading Lions

Published by Collins
An imprint of HarperCollins*Publishers*
1 London Bridge Street
London
SE1 9GF

Text and photography © Nic Bishop 2006
Design © HarperCollins*Publishers* 2006
This edition was published in 2015.

Author and photographer: Nic Bishop

British Library Cataloguing in Publication Data
A catalogue record for this publication is available from the British Library.

Designer: Sarah Elworthy
Parent notes authors: Sue Reed and Liz Webster

Printed and bound by RR Donnelley APS

www.collins.co.uk/parents